AFRICAN AMERICAN HISTORY MONTH

A Calendar of Devotions, 2003

28 Meditations of Hope, Strength, and Unity

Tyrone Gordon

Abingdon Press

African American History Month
A Calendar of Devotions 2003

Copyright © by Abingdon Press

ISBN 0-687-08083-5

Cover Photograph by Ron Benedict
MANUFACTURED IN THE UNITED STATES OF AMERICA

Introduction

Welcome to African American History Month: A Calendar of Devotions 2003! This second in the series of devotionals based on the celebrated month of culture, history, and heritage has much to offer. Inspirational messages affirming faith, spiritual growth, and community are combined with beautiful quotations from African American spirituals. Throughout the month of February, take out a few minutes of the day to reflect on the Bible reading and devotion. The power of God's love is truly evidenced in the wonderful passages for each day, insights that you will want to read again and again.

Use this book for personal reflection as well as for sharing with others in Bible study, meetings, and small groups. Like the powerful message of the gospel truth of salvation, this calendar of devotions must be spread to others in the spirit of Christ's love. Learning more about the past enables us to empower our present and therefore envision our futures for the better. And may the themes of this resource inspire and motivate us not only to promote the beautiful legacy of African Americans but also to work to strengthen family, community, and religious bodies throughout the year.

SATURDAY, FEBRUARY 1, 2003

Read: Psalm 137:1-6.

"Over my head, I hear music in the air. There must be a God somewhere!"
African American Spiritual

African Americans have been gifted by God to sing the Lord's song in the midst of a strange land. We contributed greatly to the building of this nation and paid a high cost in the process. History has taught us that we are survivors. We are overcomers. We are more than conquerors! History has taught us that no weapon that forms against us shall prosper. In the midst of injustice, racism, discrimination and mistreatment, we have been able to keep a song of hope and determination in our hearts. History has taught us how to keep on singing even when outward circumstances have played a sour note.

Often in our lives we must take up residence in a strange land. Strange lands can cause us to slip into depression and self-pity. They can make us become bitter. Our journey through strange lands can take our focus off the real goal, the Promised Land.

You are a survivor! You have in your blood the melodies of survival. Sing in the strange land. Rejoice in the strange land. Have hope in the strange land.

Prayer: Dear God, help me to hold on to hope and faith in the midst of the strange land. Amen.

Read: Genesis 16 & 21:1-21.

"I'm gonna lay down this world, gonna shoulder up my cross, gonna take it home to my Jesus, ain't that good news!"
African American Spiritual

Today declare in your spirit, "I am not a victim. I am a victor!" Say it! Shout it! Believe it! Live it! You are no longer a victim of circumstances but one who is more than a conqueror through our Lord and Savior Jesus Christ.

That is what sister Hagar from Africa declared. She would no longer play the role of a victim. Hagar was abandoned by her man. She was labeled as the "other woman." She had been mentally abused and mistreated. She was put out on her own with her son Ishmael. A single mother victimized by Abraham, Sarah, and a chauvinistic society, Hagar declared in her spirit that she would no longer allow anyone or anything to treat her like a victim.

Too often we African Americans have allowed society and others to dictate how we should feel about others and ourselves. We often play the part of the victim, a role written for us by someone else. We have been living with a victim's mentality. Well, we are not victims! We can stand tall. We can shoulder the cross.

We can face the day knowing that the One who lives in us is greater than the one who is in the world.

Prayer: Dear God, help me to remember that you are the center of my joy. Amen.

MONDAY, FEBRUARY 3, 2003

Read: Numbers 12:1-15.

> *"Walk together children, don't you get weary, there's a great camp meeting in the Promised Land."*
> African American Spiritual

We all remember those famous words by Rodney King "Can't we all just get along?" in 1992 during the uprisings in Los Angeles. The country was deeply divided by race. Not much has changed today. We are still divided by race, gender, culture, economic standing, and educational background. We still judge persons on their outward appearance. We often look upon people for what they have, wear, and drive instead of who they are in their hearts. Can't we all just get along?

In the reading for today, we have probably one of the earliest rebukes by God because of racism, prejudice, and classism. Moses' sister Miriam and brother Aaron disliked Moses' wife, an African sister named Zipporah. They had a predisposed negative attitude toward her because of her ethnicity: She was a Cushite, an Ethiopian. They caused havoc in the community by spreading their destructive racism throughout.

Hatred denies what God has created. All human beings were created in the image of God and to deny one group is a denial of what God has done. Let us strive to think more positively about others. Despite the negativity of others, I will feed only on the positive love of Christ.

Prayer: Dear God, please heal me from the effects of prejudice. Amen.

TUESDAY, FEBRUARY 4, 2003

Read: Mark 3:1-6.

> ***"Oh, fix me; oh, fix me; fix me, Jesus, fix me."***
> African American Spiritual

Many of us lead withered lives. Life experiences, society itself, and battles with racism and sexism can cause our lives to dry up. Withered dreams, withered goals, withered relationships, withered ambitions, withered self-esteem, withered purpose! We feel like the man with the withered hand that Mark describes in the reading for today.

The Lord wants us to stretch out our hands. He is the one who can bring us wholeness, healing, deliverance, salvation, and restoration. The Lord is able to restore. We only have to stretch out our hands.

First of all, don't worry about what other folks think. In the text, Jesus sees a man in need. He disregards the negative opinions and ignores the hateful vibes from the religious leaders. Restoration, healing, and deliverance can come regardless of the opinions of others.

Second, don't be afraid to make your move. Jesus tells the man with the withered hand, "Come forward!" This brother had to step out on faith. He had to make his move. Restoration will come only when you break out of the box. Make your move!

Prayer: Dear God, give me the strength to stretch out my hand to receive deliverance. Amen.

Read: 2 Corinthians 12:1-10.

> **"I know the Lord's laid his hands on me."**
> African American Spiritual

All of us struggle with something. We all have to deal with thorns in our flesh. Thorns are those things that nag and dog us everyday. Thorns are those things that keep reminding us that we don't have it going on as well as we would like to think. Thorns are those things that pull at us one way when God is trying to take us another way.

The apostle Paul had a thorn in his flesh. The thorn was painful, debilitating, and nerve-racking. The thorn kept reminding him of his limitations, and it caused him so much pain that he asked God to remove it. When God refused, Paul had to learn how to live with the thorn and to place it in proper perspective.

We need to know that thorns are not all bad. Thorns can allow us to experience God's best even when we are at our worst. Thorns cause us to rely on God's strength and God's abilities rather than our own. Paul had to learn to live with his thorn. We have to learn to live with our thorns and experience God's grace at its best.

Prayer: Dear God, help me to rely on you in the midst of the thorns of life. Amen.

Read Luke 5:4-11.

"Hush, hush, somebody's callin' my name."
African American Spiritual

There is so much more to life than what we can see. Oftentimes fears keep us in crippling circumstances. We choose to play it safe when God has called us to play it by faith. Well, what God has for us does not reside in shallow waters. Launch out into the deep. Cancel the pity party. Quit depending on others. Look into the distance with faith. The Lord is beckoning us into the deep.

Shallow water is no place for those whom God has brought from the shackles of slavery. It is no place for persons who have the capacity to soar like eagles.

Go on and let down the nets even if they are empty right now. Let down the nets even if you get knocked down in the process. Let down the nets even if narrow-minded folks put roadblocks in your way. Let down the nets even if society tries to tell you what can't be done. Let down the nets even if at first you don't succeed. Let down the nets even if you are shot down. Get up, try again, and let down the nets!

Prayer: Dear God, with your loving presence remove the fears that cripple me. Amen.

FRIDAY, FEBRUARY 7, 2003

Read Matthew 4:1-11.

"The devil can't do you no harm, when your mind is stayed on Jesus."
African American Spiritual

As a youngster, I remember the old Flip Wilson television show, which coined the phrase: *"The devil made me do it!"* The devil can't make us do anything we don't want to do. We have the power to whip the devil. We must learn to face the power of evil and to confront it on all fronts. We must come to grips with the fact that there is a power in the universe that is diametrically opposed to the will of God for this world. There is a power behind the systematic destruction of the African American male. There is a power behind the destruction of our urban centers and communities. There is a power behind every act of racism, sexism, and discrimination, and it's time to whip the devil!

If the powers of evil will attack Jesus, they will attack you and me. Hell is bent on destroying you, your self-esteem, your dreams, your aspirations, and your quality of life. Hell is bent on destroying because its job is to kill, steal, and destroy.

The Evil One has gotten wind of the great plans God has for your life. Evil will do anything and everything to distract you. It will use lies, illusions, rumor, innuendo, personal attacks, and criticism to block your forward progress. It's time to whip the devil, and the devil can be whipped. You are more than a conqueror through him who loves you. You cannot be separated from the love of God. Now come on and whip the devil!

Prayer: Dear God, in the precious name of Jesus I can stand up to the evil forces in my life. Amen.

SATURDAY, FEBRUARY 8, 2003

Read John 5:1-9.

> **"Wade in the water, wade in the water children . . .**
> **God's gonna trouble the water."**
> African American Spiritual

Sometimes years of oppression affect our thinking and how we view ourselves. We accept society's prognosis that we will never walk on our own again. We expect always to depend on hand-outs whether it is from the government or from those around us. Low self-esteem has chained many of us in the valley of ineffective living. But God is calling and even pushing us to enjoy the heights of the mountaintop. We come up with all kinds of excuses for why we don't have, what we can't do, who kept us down, and who kept us out. So often we become comfortable living with excuses.

It is time that we quit claiming defeat. It is time that we stop wallowing in failure. It is time that we stop letting other folks walk all over us and define for us who we are and what we can accomplish. It is time to stop allowing apathy to destroy our communities. Jesus is asking us a question that if answered properly could dramatically change our lives: "Do you want to be made well?"

Only we can answer the question that Jesus is posing. We must have the desire and the will to make a change. No more excuses. Just get up and get to stepping. Take up your bed and walk. You will be surprised at the strength you really do have.

Prayer: Dear God, only you define my possibilities, not society. Amen.

SUNDAY, FEBRUARY 9, 2003

Read Genesis 12:1-5.

> *"This little light of mine, I'm going to let it shine. Let it shine . . .!"*
> African American Spiritual

For five years, I served on the Board of Education in Wichita, Kansas. While serving, I would cringe and almost go under my seat to hear children labeled as "at risk." I hated that term. It told children, before they left the starting gate of life, that there would be a high probability they would fail.

Someone might have said you were at risk. You may have bought into that lie and have worn the label that society has pinned on you. Well, it is time to take it off because God has seen fit to declare that you do have a purpose. It does not matter what label others have placed on you. For when God created you, God had you in mind. In fact, God has bigger ideas for you than you even think.

However, like Abraham and Sarah, you may have to leave familiar territory. This means abandoning the familiar, relinquishing control, and putting all in the hands of God. This means venturing out into parts unknown and doing things that you did not think could be done.

Leaving comfort zones is not easy but is required in fulfilling our God-given purpose. Today, God is calling you out of the familiar and challenging you to step into new territory. Now the journey begins...

Prayer: Dear God, in order to realize your will for my life, I may have to leave my comfort zones. Amen.

Read Genesis 12: 1-5.

"Climbing up the mountain, children. Didn't here come to stay. If you never more see me again, gonna meet you at the judgment day."
African American Spiritual

Your destiny is calling. Your purpose is beckoning. It's time to begin that journey. Abraham and Sarah took a risk to venture out on only a word and a promise. It was a risky journey of faith. Leaving what we know and journeying to what we don't is indeed a risk. In the pursuit of purpose, it is a walk of faith and not one of sight.

You cannot see the future, but your response in faith will help shape it. At times there is no visible evidence of the promise, but in your spirit you feel it is there and pursue it with all your might. You feel it tugging at you. You feel it calling you. You feel it drawing you. People may think you have lost your mind, but faith is saying, "Don't give up!" Hebrews 11:8 says, "By faith Abraham obeyed when he was called to set out for a place that he was to receive as an inheritance; and he set out, not knowing where he was going."

You are going places, but it is not up to you to make or to force the way. God will find the way. God will set things in order and make things right. When you are walking in your purpose, God will always find a way to bring you through. If God brings you to it, then God will bring you through it. You are a person of purpose. There are plans for your life, your career, your ministry, your church, and your future.

Prayer: Dear God, help me to climb up the mountain, leaning on and trusting in you. Amen.

Read Genesis 37:1-11.

> *"Over my head, I hear music in the air . . .*
> *There must be a God somewhere."*
> African American Spiritual

God has planted in your mind and heart the seeds of a dream. Dreams are the mental and spiritual landscape of where God wants you to be. God's dreams permit the imagining of new possibilities and will call into question the things that are old and ready to pass away.

Joseph's dream was not ordinary. It was a dream that resonated in his spirit and connected him to God's Spirit. It caused him to align his life toward its fulfillment. The dream gave him drive and focus. He became excited about the dream. But his family could not handle it.

Arriving at your destined place will not be easy. Further, it will not take place without surviving the inevitable challenges and barriers that will be placed in the way. Not everyone with whom you come in contact will always be happy about your dream. The dream might intimidate and challenge their way of thinking and maybe change the plans they had for you. But pursue what God has planted in your mind and heart even if you have to go against the status quo. Make God's dreams your dreams.

Prayer: Dear God, you have great plans for me. Amen.

WEDNESDAY, FEBRUARY 12, 2003

Read Genesis 37:12-20.

> *"I've been 'buked and I've been scorned, I've been talked about*
> *sure as you're born."*
> African American Spiritual

In 1968 on the balcony of the Lorraine Motel, murdering bigots thought that because they had snuffed out the life of Dr. Martin Luther King, Jr., they had killed the dream of equality and opportunity for all of God's children. How mistaken they were! They did kill the dreamer, but they could not kill the dream. Why? Because you cannot kill a divinely inspired dream. You cannot stop what God is blessing. God is the fuel and the inspiration behind the seeds of the dream that have been planted in the spirit.

Joseph's brothers thought that by killing Joseph they would inevitably kill the dream. Somehow they were misguided into thinking that any human action can undermine the outcome of what has been declared by Almighty God. The dream takes a detour, but it is still very much alive.

Guard your dream because in the midst are dream killers. Society can kill your dreams by telling you that you are the wrong color, the wrong gender, or from the wrong side of town. But your dream is stronger than the greatest opposition.

Like Joseph, you might have to go to hell and back, but the dream will prevail. It comes from God, it lives through God, and it will be accomplished by the power of God.

Prayer: Dear God, thank you for the power of dreams. Amen.

THURSDAY, FEBRUARY 13, 2003

Read Genesis 42:6-9; 45:1-8.

"Tell me, how did you feel when you come out the wilderness?
Leaning on the Lord!"
African American Spiritual

Joseph had the audacity to dream big. He was committed to the dream. He was connected to the dream. He was driven by the dream! And the brother would not let anyone or anything destroy it. God has given you a dream, but you must be willing to take the necessary steps that will lead toward its fulfillment. Our dreams do not fall into our laps ready made. There are no such things as instant dreams. There is no such thing as an overnight success. The dream takes time to mature. The dream takes planning, sacrifice, and hard work. The dream takes faith. And the dream will need one of God's miracles.

God gives the dream, but we must plan and prepare for it. There are no easy short cuts to the dream; you have to be willing to pay the price and make the sacrifices in order to bring its fulfillment to pass. Some difficult choices will have to be made and sacrifices laid out so that we can align our lives to the fulfillment of God's dreams. Plan for the dream. Write down your plans and goals because a plan will keep you focused.

Be patient with the dream because God does not work in time, but God works on time. It will take suffering, setbacks, disappointments, readjustments, delayed time schedules, heartaches, and pain. But when the time is right you shall reap the seeds that you have sown. Habakkuk 2:3 says: "For there is still a [dream] for the appointed time; it speaks of the end, and does not lie. If it seems to tarry, wait for it; it will surely come, it will not delay."

Prayer: Dear God, help me to work hard for the destiny you have prepared. Amen

Read 2 Kings 5:1-14.

> **"Free at last, free at last. Thank God almighty, I'm free at last."**
> African American Spiritual

How badly do you want what God has to offer your life? How badly do we want to stomp out racism, injustice, sexism, and discrimination? How badly do we want to fulfill the mission that God has placed in our hands? How badly do we want it? These are loaded questions. How badly do you want to reach your destined place? How badly do you want to fulfill your purpose? How badly do you want to dream God's dreams?

Naaman had to answer that question for himself in the biblical text. Did he want his healing badly enough that he was willing to be obedient to the prophet's commands? Or would he allow his arrogance to come into play? Naaman's story is so much a part of our story. We want all that God has to offer but are often unwilling to do what we must to obtain it. God wants to unlock all the hidden potential and unlimited possibilities that are tucked deep inside of us. But the question is, how badly do we want it?

Sometimes we want to circumvent the road map that God has laid out for us. We want the *Reader's Digest* version of how to be blessed. We want the shortcuts when there are none. We cannot go around faithfulness. We cannot go around obedience. We cannot go around love. We cannot bypass the cross. So, now, how badly do you want it? Seek what God has for you. Whatever you have to go through will be worth it!

Prayer: Dear God, show me the path I must travel in order to do your will. Amen.

SATURDAY, FEBRUARY 15, 2003

Read 2 Corinthians 10:1-4.

"Joshua fit the battle of Jericho, and the walls came tumbling down."
African American Spiritual

We are at war. That war is not in Afghanistan or Iraq but right in our own backyards. There is a war being waged for our minds, hearts, lives, families, and communities. The war of which I speak is the *real* war on terrorism. We are fighting for our spiritual lives and sanity. We are fighting for the economic and political stability of our communities. We are fighting to bring down spiritual strongholds.

It is time to fight but we must choose our weapons carefully. Our engagements of war are different than the world's. Dr. King brought change because he and the Movement refused to stoop to the level of the enemy. Instead, they used the weapons of God to bring about change. If we choose our weapons right, together we can bring down any barrier that has been erected against us. We have the power to bring down strongholds!

It is time for us to tell the devil, "IT'S ON!" It's time to fight back. We will lose a generation if we don't fight back now. Our economic well-being is at stake; it's time to fight back. And the good news is that we already have the victory. It's on!

It's time to bring down the walls of racism. It's on! It's time to bring down the walls of violence. It's on! It's time to bring down the walls of injustice. It's on! It's time to bring down the walls of poverty. Come on, let's pull it down! It's time to put the enemy right where the enemy belongs: under our feet!

Prayer: Dear God, with you I can overcome all obstacles. Amen.

Read Daniel 3:1-26.

> *"I want Jesus to walk with me; all along my pilgrim journey,*
> *Lord, I want Jesus to walk with me."*
> African American Spiritual

We all have been through the fire: emotional fires, financial fires, relational fires, career fires, social fires. All of us have had to endure situations that were traumatic, draining, and extremely heated. We all have been in and survived the fire. Our ancestors would say, "My soul looks back and wonders how I got over." We came out because Someone was in the fire with us. Someone was there keeping us under watchful eye. Someone was there making the fire bearable. Someone was there keeping our mind in perfect peace. Someone was in the fire with us.

The three young men in the story had become victims, like so many of God's children, of racism, jealousy, and hatred. Folks hated them because of their success and accomplishments. They were singled out because they were not afraid to take a stand.

When we go through the fire we can be assured that the Lord is already there preparing for our arrival and survival. Don't let the fire scare you because the Lord has a way of taking what was meant to destroy and frustrate and use it to prove, build, and make. The Lord will use the fire to burn away the things that bind us and keep us from living the abundant life. The fire makes us strong. The fire increases our faith. The fire strengthens our determination.

Aren't you glad that when Shadrach, Meshach, and Abednego got out of the fire, the Lord stayed in? Three went in. Four were observed walking, unbound and unharmed, in the fire. But only three got out! He is still in the fire waiting for your next fiery ordeal!

Prayer: Dear God, I know you go into the fires of life with me. Amen.

MONDAY, FEBRUARY 17, 2003

Read 2 Timothy 1:1-14.

"Lord, I want to be a Christian in my heart..."
African American Spiritual

You are gifted. You are unique. After God created you, God broke the mold. You are the one and only you. God has gifted you in a very special way. Regardless of what others have said or what society has done, you are a very talented and gifted individual. You have something to offer God and society in a way no one else can. Every child of God has been empowered by the Holy Spirit to make unique contributions that will bring glory to God and help to build God's kingdom. Stir up your gift. Fan the flames of that gift. Agitate the gift. Fire up the enthusiasm of the gift. Don't shrink away from the gift. Don't hide the gift. Use the gift!

You might have been run down in your life. People may have made some ungodly predictions about who you would be and what you would become. But aren't you glad that other folks cannot determine your future and your place in God's plan? You have been crowned with glory and honor. You were created just a little lower than the angels. You are somebody! Be the best that God has created and gifted you to be. No one can be you like you. No one can do what you can do better than you! You have been spiritually and mentally equipped to move into the purpose that God has etched out for your life.

You will find fulfillment in life only when you are moving and living in your place of giftedness. You have what it takes—now take what you have and live to the glory of God. Stir up the gift!

Prayer: Dear God, in your holy name, I vow to stir up my gifts. Amen.

TUESDAY, FEBRUARY 18, 2003

Read Mark 5:21-24, 35-43.

"I will trust in the Lord, I will trust in the Lord,
I will trust in the Lord 'till I die."
African American Spiritual

When you are dealing with God, no part of life can end with a period. The Lord's actions in our lives can leave us in a state of suspense because we never know what move God will make next. The One who has the victory over death and the grave is quite capable of handling our mishaps, our crises, our setbacks, our failings, and our entrapments. Whatever the day brings, don't sign your death warrant just yet. Don't accept the negative pronouncements about your demise and downfall just yet. Tell the doubters that the predictions of your downfall have been greatly exaggerated. It isn't over until God says it's over!

However negative the experience, always hold on to hope. That is what this father did in the Gospel of Mark when it appeared his world was crumbling. Hope was all he had. Sometimes hope is all we have to hold on to. And hope will never disappoint us.

The crowd of mourners at Jarius' house laughed at Jesus because they couldn't see the possibilities. But it is never too late for hope. When faced with a crisis, don't look at it from your limited vantage point but from God's unlimited resources. See the possibilities!

Prayer: Dear God, empower me to see the positives and not the negatives in making decisions. Amen.

Read Numbers 14:1-12, 26-38.

"Every time I feel the Spirit moving in my heart, I will pray."
African American Spiritual

Can you recall any missed opportunities in your life? Did you encounter new areas in which you deeply felt a call to move in but were afraid to take that risk? So many of us have a string of missed opportunities in our lives. But today we are moving forward in order to make good on all the opportunities God places before us. You must realize that God wants us to live in the land that flows in abundance.

God never *makes* us do anything, but God will provide an open door or a window of opportunity. It is up to us to accept the challenge and seize the moment. When God opens a door of opportunity, it is up to us walk through it. We have to have the spiritual insight to realize that the time is right to move forward and to embrace the new thing that God is doing in our lives.

As we pursue God's purposes and opportunities for our lives, we must have the kind of faith that calls for us to move when God says move. God's people in Numbers were at the threshold of promise. The time was right and the window of opportunity was open, but they refused to proceed.

Don't live a life full of regret, always looking back and thinking, *I could've, should've,* or *would've!* When God says move, the timing is right. Don't be fearful. Today is your day to experience your divinely appointed opportunities. Don't miss out on your divine appointment with God-inspired opportunities. God wants to take you places. Ready! Get set! Now go!

Prayer: Dear Lord, if I stay close to you, I can pursue divine opportunities. Amen.

Read Exodus 3:1-8a.

"Sometimes I feel like a motherless child, a long ways from home."
African American Spiritual

Sometimes we are in desperate conditions. In such times we feel overwhelmed, outnumbered, and abandoned by others and even by God. The Hebrew slaves were about to break under the brutality of Egyptian slavery. Their conditions were not at all unlike what people of color still endure. Their rights had been taken away. They were being treated like second-class citizens. They were condemned to live in ghettos and government housing. Their boys were being slaughtered, beaten, and falsely incarcerated. They were forced to work for little or no money. They were about to crack under the severity of the strain. But they cried out to the Lord and discovered that God had not forgotten them. God heard their cry.

God sees our plight no matter how lonely we feel. God feels our pain. God sees our challenges. God knows our sufferings. God is intricately involved in our lives. God sees our tears. God sees our disappointments. God sees the attacks society has made upon our dignity and self-esteem. God is concerned. God has not forgotten and at this moment is preparing for our liberation!

God is coming to snatch you out of the oppressing grip and hold of the enemy. God will act. God has come down to bring deliverance. God has come down to wipe the tears from your eyes. God has come down to fight the battles that you no longer have the strength to fight. God has not forgotten you. God is about to rock your world with the deliverance and liberation you so desperately need. Help is on the way!

Prayer: Dear God, I need thee, O Lord, how I need thee. Amen.

FRIDAY, FEBRUARY 21, 2003

Read Galatians 2:15-21.

"Give me Jesus. Give me Jesus, you can have all this world, give me Jesus."
African American Spiritual

What a contradiction: death before life! We have to die in order to experience the newness of life that Christ brings to us. It is amazing how God can bring life out of death. God works within these contradictions. We have to be emptied in order to receive. We have to let go so that Christ has control. It is no longer we who live, but the Christ who lives inside us.

Daily we must go through the painful process of death so the life of Christ can be renewed and refreshed within. Every day we have to go by Calvary in order to pull off something in our lives that hinders us from being all that God has created us to be. We must be crucified with him in order to live our lives through him. There is no way for us to bypass a Calvary experience. This experience opens the door for us to move away from the powers and forces of death, decay, defeat, depression, frustration, and darkness and move more into the realm of life. In order to experience the benefits of the resurrection we have to face Good Friday.

The Lord offers us lives filled with victory, possibilities, and transformation only by way of the cross. Before we go any further, let's go to the cross. Let's crucify those bad attitudes. Let's crucify negative thinking. Let's crucify destructive behavior. Let's crucify those bad ties and relationships that mean us no good. Let's go by Calvary so that the life of Christ can live in us unhindered in its fullness.

Prayer: Dear God, fill me with your holy presence. Amen.

Read 1 Kings 19:1-15a.

"I've been in the storm so long, oh, give me a little time to pray,
I've been in the storm too long."
African American Spiritual

All of us battle spirits of discouragement and depression from time to time. Those are the times when we question our purpose and our destiny. Bad news, divorce, the ending of a long-term relationship, death, sickness, unemployment, and failure can cause us to go into the deep and dark caves of retreat.

This is the place Elijah found himself—in a cave, a place of mental and spiritual depression. He was burned out and stressed out. He was on the run for his life. Jezebel places a bounty on his head, and Elijah finds himself intimidated, suicidal, self-righteous, and in hiding. That was no place for him.

We often end up in places where we don't belong emotionally, mentally, spiritually, and physically as well. Like Elijah we are on the run. My word for you is don't run and hide because you will end up in places where you don't belong.

Cancel your pity party and come on out of that cave. Quit feeling sorry for yourself. If you stay in the cave too long, your perception of reality will become skewed. You will not see things as they really are. Stop raking yourself over the coals for mistakes of the past. There are new opportunities for the future. Come on out of the cave. It's lonely in the cave. It's cold in the cave. You will be reminded of your defeats and failures in the cave. Come out of the cave!

Prayer: Dear God, there is light at the end of the tunnel. Amen.

SUNDAY, FEBRUARY 23, 2003

Read Ephesians 3:14-21.

"O when the saints go marching in, O when the saints go marching in, O Lord, I want to be in that number when the saints go marching in."
African American Spiritual

C an't you feel the winds of change blowing in your life today? God is about to do a new thing. The atmosphere for miracles is developing, and the growing pangs are beginning to be felt. These are the signs that a new move of God is about to take place in your life. These are the signs that God is getting you ready for the next level. You are standing at the dawn of a new day, a day that your ancestors dreamed about, a day they prayed about, a day they sacrificed for so you could enjoy it. Today is the first day of the best days of your life. You are going places because your season has come!

God has made it clear that God's ways are not our ways. God has no limits. God has no boundaries. You are a person of purpose and great things are ready to explode within. No matter what others say, the time is now to make your move. Go for it! You are going places because God is getting ready to bless you beyond imagination. You are going places because God has already gone before you and prepared the way. You are going places because God has set this thing in motion and has already worked it out. You are going places because God's power is at work in your life!

Prayer: Dear God, thanks to your grace, new and blessed changes are coming my way. Amen.

MONDAY, FEBRUARY 24, 2003

Read John 15:1-7.

"I shall not, I shall not be moved, I shall not, I shall not be moved. Just like a tree that's planted by the water, I shall not be moved."
African American Spiritual

Our ancestors stayed strong in the midst of adversity because they stayed connected to the source of their strength. That is how they could be like a tree planted by the waters, with roots deep and strong. They could not be shaken because they were connected. We need to learn that lesson. We need to stay connected to the source of our lives. We have gotten so caught up in the rat race that we often neglect the feeding of our souls. Unlike our ancestors we can be moved by every wind and storm that comes along because we have failed to realize the definition of the vine and the branches.

Jesus is the vine. God is the gardener. We are the branches. It does not take a rocket scientist to figure out what happens to a branch that is disconnected from the vine. In order to walk into our purpose, we must stay connected to the One who nourishes and feeds us. God's future for us is filled with power, possibilities, and productivity, but in order to reach that future we must stay connected to the Vine. It would be spiritual suicide to be disengaged from our source of power, growth, and life.

As we stay connected, we continue to grow because we abide in him. We branch out. We step out. We come out into our own! If we are not growing, then we are dead or dying. The Lord expects us to bear fruit. God is glorified when we live productive and helpful lives of service. We can stay strong only if we stay connected.

Prayer: Dear God, you are the vine and I am the branch. Amen.

TUESDAY, FEBRUARY 25, 2003

Read Philippians 4:7-9.

"I woke up this morning with my mind, stayed on Jesus!
Hallelu, Hallelu, Hallelujah!"
African American Spiritual

All of us have heard the familiar slogan of the College Fund: "A mind is a terrible thing to waste." What a true statement. Our minds can do us good or they can do us harm. Our minds can inspire us or sabotage us. We will act out what we think about ourselves.

The battleground for your victory and success will be in your mind. Our mental stability is key to our well-being and success. Paul admonishes us to take proper care of our minds. Everything we ever can be or achieve begins in our minds. Our potential is in our minds. Our drive to be the best is in our minds. Our desire to please God comes from our minds. God works through our minds. As a person thinks, so they are, Jesus teaches.

Be careful of what you put in your mind. Whatever you put in is what will show up in your life. Occupy your mind with elevated thoughts and not gutter thoughts, positive thoughts and not negative thoughts, spiritual thoughts and not carnal thoughts. If you feed and thrive on negativity, then your life will be negative and unbearable.

Let the Lord guard your mind. Keep your mind in good hands. You will find no better hands than those of the Lord. If you feed your mind on the things of God, then God will guard your mind from the negative attacks of the powers of hell that wish to defeat you. God will keep you in perfect peace when your mind is stayed on the Lord. It's all in your mind.

Prayer: Dear God, my mind is kept in perfect peace when it rests in you. Amen.

WEDNESDAY, FEBRUARY 26, 2003

Read Luke 12:13-21.

> *"Have you got good religion? Certainly, Lord!"*
> African American Spiritual

African Americans spend billions of dollars annually on things we don't need, trying to impress. We have bought into the commercial hype that we are worth the car we drive, the clothes we wear, and where we live. We have let things rule us instead of us ruling things. But in order to live the abundant life to its fullness, we have to get our priorities right. Many people today live with misplaced priorities.

Jesus talks more about our handling of money than many other things. He clearly knew that how we view money would have a direct bearing on how we live and how we show our love for God. What are your priorities? Are you overextending yourself trying to make a living? Or are you trying to make a life?

When our priorities are misplaced we begin to let what we have define who we are. We live in a society that is fascinated with the rich and famous. Everybody wants to be "like Mike." We judge persons from their outward appearance instead of the content of their character. When our priorities are in order we are comfortable with ourselves because we know that we are children of the Most High God. You are not what you drive. You are not what you wear. You are who God says you are. You are somebody whether you are broke or have money in your pocket. You are defined by who you are in the kingdom of God.

Prayer: Dear God, show me the way to live a life that honors you. Amen.

THURSDAY, FEBRUARY 27, 2003

Read 1 Samuel 1:4-19.

"Nobody knows the trouble I've seen, nobody knows my sorrow;
Nobody knows the trouble I've seen, glory, hallelujah!"
African American Spiritual

Have you ever been through those barren times in life when everything seems to be on hold? Nothing seems to be coming to birth or fruition. No victory. No success. No forward movement. Dreams are crashing, the walls are closing in. Your confidence and self-esteem are shaken. Your life is filled with a whole lot of drama. You are at the point where Hannah was, and you can't take it anymore! Her rival Peninnah was fertile and she was barren. Peninnah rubbed it in, and it messed with Hannah's mind. For the culture of her day, Hannah's barrenness was a social embarrassment and she couldn't take the ridicule any longer.

Our barren times are when we are most vulnerable, when we feel empty and alone. Hannah was struggling with God's timing, and don't we do the same? Just because we are at a standstill does not mean we aren't going anywhere. Just because a plane is in a holding pattern does not mean it will not eventually land. Standing still may be God's way of telling us that the timing is not right. It can be a time of preparation, a time of growth, and most definitely a time of prayer. We should take our burdens to the Lord and leave them there.

God will remember us. We never again hear the name Peninnah in the Scriptures, but God remembers Hannah. She gives birth to Samuel, the last judge in Israel and the first prophet and priest to the first king, Saul. The Lord remembered Hannah and the Lord will remember you.

Prayer: Dear God, my barren places will turn fruitful if I wait on you. Amen.

FRIDAY, FEBRUARY 28, 2003

Read Jeremiah 29:1-14.

"There's a better day a comin', fare ye well, fare ye well. There's a better day a comin', fare ye well, fare ye well . . ."
African American Spiritual

This month has been a great journey for us. I hope you know now that you are going places. You are a child of destiny! God has great and wonderful plans for you. You have not reached your final destination in life yet. There is a divine purpose for your life. You have a calling for your life. You have a destiny to fulfill. God wants to do something incredibly glorious in your life. God wants to be involved in the making of your future. Celebrate the fact that you are a marked child of destiny.

God's plans are for good and not to harm. God's plans are to prosper, not to destroy. God's plans are to lift up, not to put down. So don't let anything or anyone reroute you from the destiny that has been declared by divine decree. God has spoken unlimited possibilities and opportunities into your life. When you are told that you can't—you say, "Oh yes I can!" When you are told that you won't—you say, "Oh yes I will!" When you are told you don't have what it takes—you say, "Oh yes I do!" God is ordering your steps and you do have an appointment with destiny. Through your failures, your mistakes, your past, and your mess, God is still speaking into your life a future with hope. The mishaps of today and yesterday will not be the final word on your tomorrow. Get moving! You have an appointment with destiny because you are destiny's child.

Prayer: Dear God, thank you for my destiny. I can do all things through Christ who strengthens me. Amen.